MY FIRST GERMAN BOOK

GERMAN-ENGLISH BOOK
FOR BILINGUAL CHILDREN

 www.RaisingBilingualChildren.com

D1519081

DEUTSCHES

der **ALLIGATOR**
Alligator

die **BALLOON**
Balloon

der **COMPUTER**
Computer

die **GABEL**
Fork

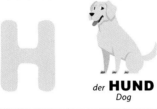

der **HUND**
Dog

der **IGEL**
Hedgehog

die **MILCH**
Milk

die **NASE**
Nose

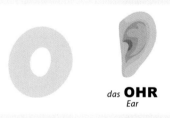

das **OHR**
Ear

die **SOCKE**
Sock

der **TISCH**
Table

die **UHR**
Clock

der **YACHT**
Yacht

das **ZEBRA**
Zebra

die **ÄPFEL**
Apples

ALPHABET

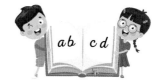

D
der **DINOSAURIER**
Dinosaur

E
das **EIS**
Ice

F
das **FLUSSPFERD**
Hippopotamus

J
die **JACKE**
Jacket

K
das **KÄNGURU**
Kangaroo

L
der **LÖWE**
Lion

P
der **PAPAGEI**
Parrot

Q
der **QUALLE**
Jellyfish

R
die **RAKETE**
Rocket

V
der **VOGEL**
Bird

W
die **WASSERMELONE**
Watermelon

X
das **XYLOPHON**
Xylophone

Ö
das **ÖL**
Oil

Ü
die **ÜBERRASCHUNG**
Surprise

ß
der **FUß**
Foot

WILDE TIERE

die **GIRAFFE**
Giraffe

der **ELEFANT**
Elephant

das **ZEBRA**
Zebra

der **STRAUSS**
Ostrich

der **HIRSCH**
Deer

der **BÄR**
Bear

der **LÖWE**
Lion

der **FUCHS**
Fox

DOMESTIZIERTE TIERE

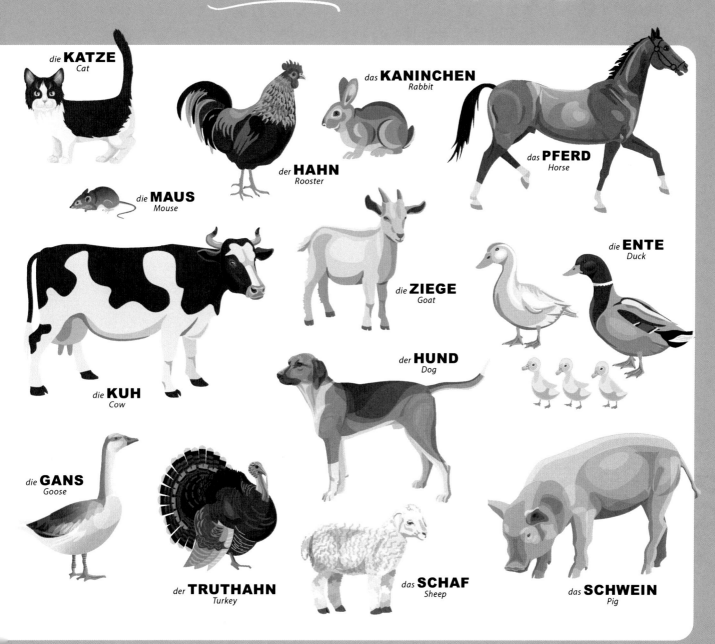

die **KATZE**
Cat

der **HAHN**
Rooster

das **KANINCHEN**
Rabbit

das **PFERD**
Horse

die **MAUS**
Mouse

die **ZIEGE**
Goat

die **ENTE**
Duck

die **KUH**
Cow

der **HUND**
Dog

die **GANS**
Goose

der **TRUTHAHN**
Turkey

das **SCHAF**
Sheep

das **SCHWEIN**
Pig

FORMEN

der **KREISE**

Circle

das **QUADRAT**

Square

das **DREIECK**

Triangle

das **RECHTECK**

Rectangle

der **RHOMBUS**

Rhombus

das **OVAL**

Oval

SHAPES

das HERZ

Heart

der STERN

Star

das KREUZ

Cross

der PFEIL

Arrow

das PENTAGON

Pentagon

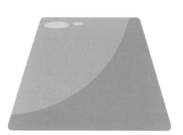

das TRAPEZ

Trapezoid

FRÜCHTE | FRUITS

der **APFEL**
Apple

die **BANANE**
Banana

die **ANANAS**
Pineapple

die **APRIKOSE**
Apricot

die **PFLAUME**
Plum

die **BIRNE**
Pear

die **ORANGE**
Orange

die **ZITRONE**
Lemon

BEEREN |

die **ERDBEERE**
Strawberry

die **WASSERMELONE**
Watermelon

die **TRAUBE**
Grape

die **KIRSCHE**
Cherry

die **HEIDELBEERE**
Blueberry

die **HIMBEERE**
Raspberry

der **GRANATAPFEL**
Pomegranate

der **KIWI**
Kiwi

GEMÜSE

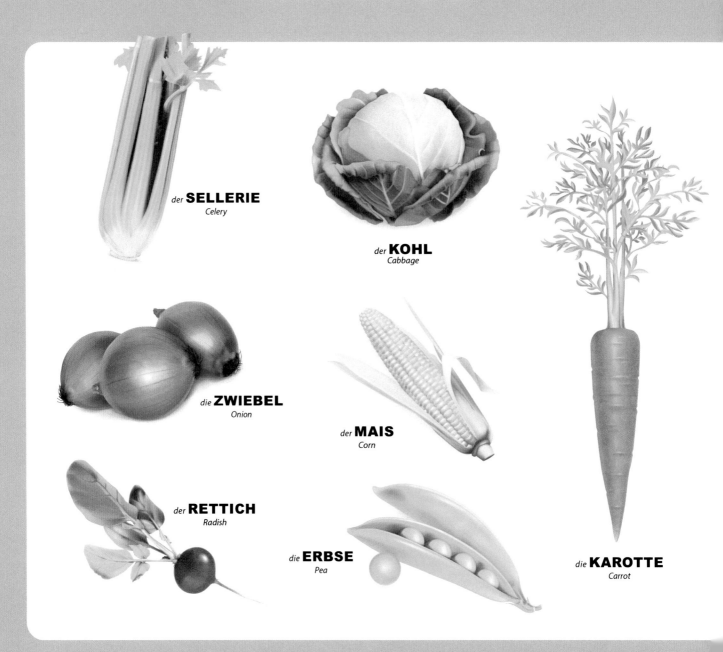

der **SELLERIE**
Celery

der **KOHL**
Cabbage

die **ZWIEBEL**
Onion

der **MAIS**
Corn

der **RETTICH**
Radish

die **ERBSE**
Pea

die **KAROTTE**
Carrot

VEGETABLES

die **BROKKOLI**
Broccoli

der **KNOBLAUCH**
Garlic

der **SPARGEL**
Asparagus

die **RÜBE**
Beet

die **ARTISCHOCKE**
Artichoke

die **KARTOFFELN**
Potato

der **SPINAT**
Spinach

die **LAUCHZWIEBEL**
Scallion

ZAHLEN

ZWEI
Two

EIN
One

DREI
Three

VIER
Four

FÜNF
Five

SECHS
Six

NUMBERS

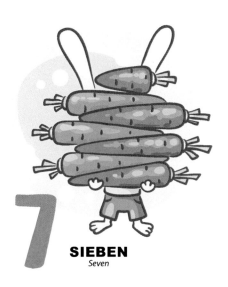

7

SIEBEN
Seven

8

ACHT
Eight

9

NEUN
Nine

10

ZEHN
Ten

FARBEN

ROT

 die **TOMATE**
Tomato

 der **MARIENKÄFER**
Ladybug

 der **KREBS**
Crab

 *die* **ROSE**
Rose

GELB

 *der* **KÄSE**
Cheese

 *die* **BIENE**
Bee

 *der* **WEIZEN**
Wheat

 die **SONNENBLUME**
Sunflower

COLORS

GRÜN

 das **BLATT**
Leaf

 der **FROSCH**
Frog

 die **GURKE**
Cucumber

 die **AVOCADO**
Avocado

BLAU

 der **WAL**
Whale

 der **SCHMETTERLING**
Butterfly

 die **JEANS**
Jeans

 der **FISCH**
Fish

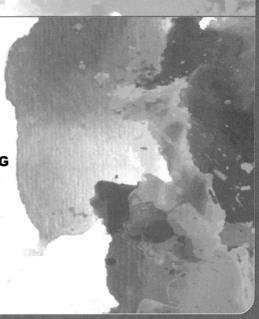

JAHRESZEITEN

der **WINTER**
Winter

der **FRÜHLING**
Spring

SEASONS

der **SOMMER**
Summer

der **HERBST**
Autumn

MEIN HAUS

DIE KÜCHE

der TELLER
Plate

der **LÖFFEL**
Spoon

die **GABEL**
Fork

die TASSE
Cup

die **TEEKANNE**
Teapot

der **VORRATSTOPF**
Stock pot

DAS KINDERZIMMER

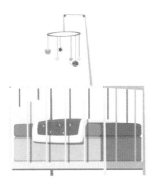

das **KINDERBETT**
Crib

die **BLÖCKE**
Blocks

die **PUPPE**
Doll

die **STAPELRINGE**
Stacking rings

MY HOUSE

DAS BADEZIMMER

die **ZAHNBÜRSTE**

Toothbrush

die **BADEWANNE**

Bathtub

das **HANDTUCH**

Towel

das **WASCHBECKEN**

Sink

DAS WOHNZIMMER

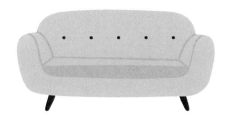

das **SOFA**

Couch

der **SESSEL**

Armchair

die **LAMPE**

Lamp

das **FERNSEHEN**

TV

BERUFE

der **GESCHÄFTSMANN**
Businessman

die **ÄRZTIN**
Doctor

der **FEUERWEHRMANN**
Firefighter

die **KÖCHIN**
Cook

die **LEHRERIN**
Teacher

der **PROGRAMMIERER**
Programmer

PROFESSIONS

der **POLIZIST**
Policeman

die **ASTRONAUTIN**
Astronaut

die **MALERIN**
Artist

der **MUSIKER**
Musician

der **FUßBALLSPIELER**
Soccer Player

der **FARMER**
Farmer

TRANSPORT

TRANSPORTATION

das **FLUGZEUG**
Airplane

der **HUBSCHRAUBER**
Helicopter

der **HEIßLUFTBALLON**
Hot Air Balloon

die **VERKEHRSAMPEL**
Traffic light

das **AUTO**
Car

der **LKW**
Truck

das **FAHRRAD**
Bike

das **MOTORRAD**
Motorcycle

das **FEUERWEHRAUTO**
Fire truck

der **BUS**
Bus

der **KRANKENWAGEN**
Ambulance

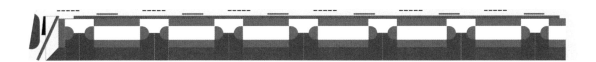

der **ZUG**
Train

TIERGERÄUSCHE

KATZE
MIAUT
MIAU

HUND
BELLT
WUFF

FROSCH
QUAKT
RIBBIT

HAHN
KRÄHT
COCK-A-DOODLE-DOO

GANS
HUPT
HONK

ENTEN
QUACKS
QUACK

ANIMAL SOUNDS

KUH
MOOS
MOO

PFERDE
WIEHERN
WIEHERN

SCHWEIN
SCHNAUBT
OINK-OINK

ZIEGE
MECKERT
BAA

ESEL
SCHREI
HEE-HAW

BIENE
SUMMT
BUZZ

GEGENSÄTZE

GROß
Big

KLEIN
Small

SAUBER
Clean

DRECKIG
Dirty

HEIß
Hot

KALT
Cold

TAG
Day

NACHT
Night

OPPOSITES

HOCH
Tall

KURZ
Short

GEÖFFNET
Opened

GESCHLOSSEN
Closed

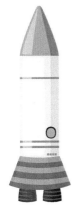 

LANGE
Long

KURZ
Short

VOLL
Full

LEER
Empty

Thank you very much

It would be amazing if you wrote
an honest review on Amazon!
It means so much to us!

Questions?
Email us hello@RaisingBilingualChildren.com

Anna Young

www.RaisingBilingualChildren.com

Edition 1.0 - Last updated on August 8, 2021

Made in the USA
Monee, IL
11 February 2022

91111494R00019